Board of Education v. Pico (1982)

By JOHN COOPERSMITH GOLD

TWENTY-FIRST CENTURY
BOOKS
A Division of
Henry Holt and Company

New York

To Susan, without whom this would not have been possible.

Twenty-First Century Books
A Division of Henry Holt and Company, Inc.
115 West 18th Street
New York, NY 10011

Henry Holt® and colophon are trademarks of
Henry Holt and Company, Inc.
Publishers since 1866

Library of Congress Cataloging-in-Publication Data
Gold, John Coopersmith.
Board of Education v. Pico (1982) : book banning / John Coopersmith Gold. — 1st ed.
p. cm. — (Supreme Court decisions)
Includes bibliographical references and index.
1. Pico, Steven A.—Trials, litigation, etc.—Juvenile literature. 2. Island Trees Public Schools (Levittown, N.Y.)—
Trials, litigation, etc.—Juvenile literature. 3. School libraries—Censorship—United States—Juvenile literature.
[1. Island Trees Public Schools (Levittown, N.Y.)—Trials, litigation, etc. 2. Censorship. 3. School libraries.
4. Libraries.]
I. Title. II. Series: Supreme Court decisions (New York, N.Y.).
KF228.P45G65 1994b   344.73'0531— dc20   94-21861
[347.304531]   CIP AC

Photo Credits
Photos on pages 24, 44, and 63 courtesy of Edna Yarris
Photo on page 52 courtesy of Barbara Bernstein, New York Civil Liberties Union
Photo on page 83 courtesy of Michael Dishnow
All other photos provided by AP / Wide World Photos

Design
Tina Tarr-Emmons

Typesetting and Layout
Custom Communications

ISBN 0-8050-3660-1
First Edition 1994

Printed in Mexico
All first editions are printed on acid-free paper ∞.
10 9 8 7 6 5 4 3 2 1

Contents

Banned in Boston

cen-sor n. 1. an authorized examiner of literature, plays, or other material, who may prohibit what he considers morally or otherwise objectionable. cen-sor-ship n. 1. the act or process of censoring.
—The American Heritage Dictionary

Book censorship has been around for as long as people have been putting their thoughts in writing for the public. As early as 387 B.C. the philosopher Plato suggested that the works of Homer, a Greek poet, be edited for younger readers because certain parts of the books were not appropriate for them.

This process of cutting out objectionable parts of books is also called Bowdlerization, after Thomas Bowdler, a 19th-century doctor. Bowdler believed certain passages in the works of English playwright and poet William Shakespeare were not suitable for family reading. So Bowdler removed those passages that were, in his words, "unfit to be read aloud by a gentleman in the company of ladies," and in 1818 he published the ten-volume *Family Shakespeare*.[1]

During the Civil War, many Southerners objected to the use of geography books in schools that described to children the North as more important than the South. Others were unhappy with books that were critical of slavery in the South.[2]

In the late 1800s and early 1900s a group of people in Boston became concerned by the language in certain books and formed the Watch and Ward Society for the Suppression of Vice. This group formed an alliance with booksellers and newspaper publishers in the city to prevent the sale of books they considered unsuitable because they violated Victorian moral codes, now viewed as being stuffy and hypocritical.[3] Members of the society acted as undercover agents and tried to buy the books at bookstores. If they succeeded, they had the bookseller arrested. By 1928 the group had managed to ban more than 100 titles from bookstores in the city. Those books included *The Sun Also Rises* by Ernest Hemingway and *Mosquitoes* by William Faulkner. The group eventually fell out of favor after some people began questioning its undercover methods. By 1931 the group was no longer a force in Boston.

Censorship in the Schools

Attempts to censor books read by schoolchildren began in earnest after World War II. After the war, classroom instruction became more standardized as schools all across the country began teaching similar material to their students. Most of the material was noncontroversial. But as society changed, so did the material taught to students. In the 1960s textbooks and classroom teachers began to introduce controversial ideas. They discussed changes in society, the expanding role of women in the workforce, and the treatment of

Nancy Mitchell, an English teacher in Anaheim, California, looks at a pile of paperback books on her desk in 1978. The books were banned from the classroom because they were deemed inappropriate for high-school students. The book *Black Boy* by Richard Wright was one of the books banned by the Island Trees School Board in Long Island, New York.

7

minorities. The books also included criticism of the United States. Teachers encouraged students to take a critical look at the world and to question their views and the views of their parents.[4]

Some parents objected to what they read in their children's textbooks and in the books their children found in the school library. Most of their objections centered on the language—vulgar words or slang—used in the books. The parents did not want their children to use such language. But in some cases, the objectionable words were important to the meaning of the book.

One book that has been banned by several school boards is *Down These Mean Streets*, by Piri Thomas. The book describes the life of a young boy growing up in Spanish Harlem, a neighborhood in New York City. The author uses the words he grew up with to describe his experiences. Some parents are unhappy about the use of those words and the graphic situations the author describes. Other parents and students believe it is important for students to be able to read the book because it describes a life they otherwise would not know.

In a similar case, a school in Maine tried to ban *365 Days*, a book about soldiers wounded in Vietnam. The soldiers, in great pain, use four-letter words in the book. When the case went to trial, Vietnam veterans told the judge that the book would be meaningless if the objectionable words were deleted.

Even the dictionary has been challenged by parents. In April 1977 a school board in Eldon, Missouri, voted to remove *The American Heritage Dictionary* from the junior high school. The vote came after 24 parents filed a complaint that said 39 words in the book were objectionable.

People who oppose censorship say it is important for children to read different views, even if those views do not agree with their own or those of their parents. The American Library Association supports the right of students and other people to read what they choose. In its "Freedom to Read Statement," the ALA states:

The power of a democratic system to adapt to
change is vastly strengthened by the freedom of its
citizens to choose widely from among conflicting
opinions offered freely to them.

This book is about a lawsuit filed because a school board tried to control
what its students could read in the school libraries. The board members said
certain books should be removed from the libraries because they found them
offensive. Although the board members said they were not censors, they acted
like censors.

The board's action was challenged by students and their parents in court.
They said the board did not have the power to remove the books. The results
of that lawsuit—*Board of Education v. Pico*—still have an effect today.

Island Trees School Board vice president Frank Martin, left, and board president Richard Ahrens. The two men led the fight to remove books from the school library.

CHAPTER ONE

Off the Shelves

We must emphasize the fact that what we are talking about here is not censorship. . . . What we are talking about is excluding objectionable reading material from our school libraries.[1]

— **Island Trees School Board**

In June 1982, nine books were returned to the shelves of the junior high-school and senior high-school libraries in the Island Trees Union Free School District No. 26 on Long Island, New York. Their return came more than six years after their removal had been ordered by the school board. It ended what some have called one of the most significant schoolbook censorship cases in U.S. history and marked a victory for the right of students to read whatever they choose.

The case began on the autumn night of November 7, 1975, when two members of the district's school board slipped away from the senior high school's Winter School Night, a sporting event. The board members, Frank Martin and school board president Richard Ahrens, asked a janitor to open the door to the school's library.

There Martin and Ahrens checked the titles of the books in the library's index file against those on a list Martin was carrying. The list had names of books that a parents' group in upstate New York had said were not suitable for children. The two men discovered nine books in the library that matched the titles on their list.

While they were checking the books, the high-school principal, Irving Carroll, looked in and asked what they were doing. They told him, and he left.

More than three months later, on February 24, 1976, members of the Island Trees School Board met with Carroll. Joining Martin and Ahrens on the board were Christina Fasulo, Patrick Hughes, Richard Melchers, Richard Michaels, and Louis Nessim. The board members also met with Ernest Valenze, principal of the district's junior high school, and Richard Morrow, superintendent of the school district. The meeting took place after the regular school board meeting. The board members told the principals to remove the nine books on the list from the library shelves and bring them to the board's office. They said they wanted to read the books themselves.

Morrow told board members he believed they were making a mistake and said the board should follow a policy it had approved for reviewing books. That policy called for the board to appoint a committee to review the books in question and to make a recommendation.

Books Are Removed

The next day, the nine books were removed from the library shelves. A tenth book, found in the junior high-school library, was also removed. An eleventh book being used in a senior high-school English class was removed as well. All the books were taken to Morrow's office.

The book removal worried Morrow. He knew the board and the school could get in trouble for removing the books. So he kept the books in his office and wrote a memo to the board members, hoping to change their minds.

On February 27, three days after the meeting, Morrow sent the board his memo. In it he warned the board that removing the books without following the review process would create a "furious uproar, not only in the district, but across the community, Long Island, and the state. I don't believe you want such an uproar and I certainly don't."[2] Morrow also warned the board members that the issue was "heating up" and that copies of the list were being circulated.

The board ignored Morrow's warning. On March 3, Ahrens sent Morrow a memo asking again for the books. The books were placed in the school board's office.

The books removed from the two libraries were *Slaughterhouse Five* by Kurt Vonnegut; *The Fixer* by Bernard Malamud; *The Naked Ape* by Desmond Morris; *Down These Mean Streets* by Piri Thomas; *Best Short Stories by Negro Writers*, edited by Langston Hughes; *A Hero Ain't Nothing but a Sandwich* by Alice Childress; *Soul on Ice* by Eldridge Cleaver; *A Reader for Writers*, edited by Jerome Archer; *Go Ask Alice*, author anonymous; *Laughing Boy* by Oliver LaFarge; and *Black Boy* by Richard Wright. Two of the books, *The Fixer* and *Laughing Boy*, had won Pulitzer Prizes.

The list had come from a conference Martin, Ahrens, and a third board member, Patrick Hughes, had attended in Watkins Glen, New York, earlier that fall. The conference was sponsored by a conservative parents' group called Parents of New York, United (PONY-U). The group was concerned about laws regarding education in New York State and with the kinds of books students were reading.

The list included short excerpts from the books the parents' group thought were unsuitable. The excerpts contained mostly vulgar language, discussions of sexual intercourse, and, in some cases, phrases PONY-U and the board members considered "anti-Christian." For example, they noted a line in

Vonnegut's book in which one character calls Jesus Christ "a bum." The group thought that passage was offensive to Christians.

In *A Hero Ain't Nothing but a Sandwich*, a black teacher tells his students that George Washington owned slaves. The board members said this was "anti-American." Morris's *The Naked Ape* contains graphic discussions of sexual intercourse. *Go Ask Alice*, a book written by a teenage girl who was hooked on drugs and alcohol, contains vulgar four-letter words. It also has descriptions of drug users and talks about sexual experiences. Going on down the list, board members said *The Fixer* was "anti-Semitic" — hurtful to Jewish people. The book's author, however, notes the book is actually a defense of the Jews in czarist Russia.

As the Island Trees School Board was removing the 11 books from the shelves of its school libraries, other schools and parents were wrestling with the same issue.

During the 1970s and early 1980s many people challenged the types of books read by students in public schools. Most of those challenges came from people who argued that public schools had two duties. One was to teach the students basic skills, like reading, writing, and mathematics. The second was to transmit certain moral values to students. These values, they said, should reflect the values of the community in which the students lived.

Many parents at this time were concerned that their children were reading and discussing certain topics in school. These topics included communism, civil rights, sexuality, and moral values. They had not been discussed in schools before and reflected changes in American society at the time.

In some cases, the disputes were taken to court. The judges who heard these cases made different rulings, although generally they supported a limited power of school boards to determine what books are allowed in a school library.[3] The judges agreed, however, that the courts should usually stay out of local school matters. They also agreed with people who said local schools should reflect the values of the communities they served.

In a 1980 decision on a Warsaw, Indiana, schoolbook-banning case, the justices for the Seventh Circuit Court of Appeals stated:

> It is generally permissible and appropriate for
> local boards to make educational decisions based
> upon their personal, social, political, and moral
> values.[4]

In the *Pico* case, the members of the Island Trees School Board believed it was their responsibility to remove the books. They said the books offended their personal moral values. These values, they said, were shared by members of the Island Trees community who had elected the board members. Because of this, the board claimed it had the power to remove the books.

Author Kurt Vonnegut poses with a stack of the books removed from the school libraries by the Island Trees School Board. One of his books, *Slaughterhouse Five,* was among the books involved in the banning.

CHAPTER TWO

The Controversy Grows

You remind me of kids standing on the corner, passing a book around and saying, "Look at page 30, line 5."[1]

— **Julius Seide**
Island Trees resident

As Superintendent Morrow had warned, people soon learned of the board's action. By mid-March, everyone in the community and many in the state knew about the removal of the books. And many were not happy.

At a meeting on March 19, 1976, board members tried to explain to the public their reasons for removing the books. They said the books contained material "which is offensive to Christians, Jews, Blacks and Americans in general." They went on to say that the books contained "obscenities, blasphemies, brutality, and perversion beyond description."[2]

The board's explanation did not satisfy the people who attended the meeting. One member of the audience, resident Edna Yarris, who had a child in the high school, told the board members their actions reminded her of book burnings in Nazi Germany.[3]

On March 22, Yarris invited a group of people to her home to talk about the ban. She wanted people to take action that would return the books to the libraries. Although she invited only a few people to the meeting, more than 50, including some students, attended. In addition to discussing the ban, the group collected $77.25 to pay for possible legal fees. The group also decided to file a protest with the state education commissioner and to begin a campaign to get other residents involved in the issue. Yarris urged everyone to come to a March 30 school board meeting to protest the ban.

The board's action was also criticized by many newspapers in the area. An editorial in the *New York Times* eight days later criticized the board members, noting they had not read the books before removing them and questioning the board's motives.

"The real target of book censors," the editorial read, "is the changing world of modern social behavior and language, rather than the unread volumes on the shelf." The writer went on to say that parents had a right to monitor their own children's reading at home, "but have no right to tell other parents what their children may or may not read."[4]

A cartoon published in the *New York Daily News* portrayed two school board members as shady hoods, sneaking into the library to snatch books.

Many residents wrote letters to local newspapers. Most of the letters criticized the board and the book ban. One parent said the ban would actually encourage students to read the books. Others said they had read the books and found they contained valuable lessons.

Board Members Convinced

Despite the criticism, school board members remained convinced they had done the right thing. In interviews with newspaper reporters that month, board members said they believed their decision to remove the books was correct.

They said it was their job to reflect the values of the community in which they lived.

"This is our responsibility," board member Hughes told a *New York Times* reporter in a March 28 story. "We are supposed to review what happens in our schools."[5]

"We feel we have to draw the line somewhere," school board president Ahrens told the same reporter. Ahrens stated later that he objected to the books because of the "obscenity and bad taste" contained in them. He also said the books were irrelevant to the district's basic course of study.[6]

The board used the March 1976 newsletter it sent to families in the school district to defend its action. In that newsletter the board accused its critics of lying about the facts of the issue. The board also accused critics of the ban of trying to take power away from the parents of the school district.

"The next question is, who makes the decision?" the newsletter article asked. "Does the news media decide from which books your children are taught? Should it be the people who award Pulitzer Prizes? Or maybe it should be today's dedicated teacher union leaders? We believe that not even the professional educators and educational administrators have a right to usurp the parents' authority in these matters."[7]

Angry Meeting

Despite the board's efforts to justify its actions, many in the community continued to protest the book ban. At the meeting on March 30—the second since the board's action became public—more than 500 people filled the Island Trees High School auditorium. Most were there to protest the removal of the books.

Among those in the audience were students who said they thought the book removal was wrong. "These books are very tame," one student said. "It's nothing you can't hear in the sixth-grade school bus." Other students said the books exposed them to people and ways of life not seen in their sheltered community.[8]

William Connolly, a New York City firefighter, agreed. "I've heard worse language working in the ghetto, and my sons have heard worse playing ice hockey," he said. "I'm a fireman in South Jamaica and I used to be a city cop, which would probably surprise some of these people on the board, and I'm an Irishman who grew up in New York City. That's supposed to make me conservative, according to writers and other people who live in New York City. But we're all not stupid out here. I think this board is wrong—and so does the majority of people in this district."[9]

Rising to speak, School Superintendent Morrow criticized the school board for bypassing its own book review process. That process called for books to be chosen by librarians after consulting with teachers and students. Citizens who objected to a particular book were supposed to put their complaints in writing and send them to the superintendent, who would appoint a committee to review the book.

Morrow also criticized the board for judging the books without reading them first. He noted that the board removed the books using a list prepared for a group outside the community and that board members did not consider the views of the community when they made their decision.

Not Censors

Many of the people who criticized the board's action called them censors. But the board members denied that they were censoring the books. They said the books might not belong in a school library, but they could be found in the community's public library.

"If you want to tell your child about this wonderful book you can take her

20

to the public library," said Ahrens. "I would not dream of trying to take that book out of the public library. That would be censorship—and we are not censors."[10]

That sentiment was also in a press release the board issued on March 19, after the members were criticized by residents and in the media for removing the books.

"This Board of Education wants to make it clear that we in no way are book banners or book burners. While most of us agree that these books have a place on the shelves of the public library, we all agree that these books simply do not belong in school libraries, where they are so easily accessible to children whose minds are still in the formative stage and where their presence actually entices children to read and savor them."[11]

Community Values

The board's strongest defense was that it was acting to protect the values of the community it represented. Ahrens said he was "basically a conservative in my general philosophy and feel that the community I represent as a school board member shares that philosophy."[12]

Everyone agreed that the Island Trees community was a conservative one. In 1976 the district covered about 5,000 homes in Nassau County in the towns of Bethpage, Plainedge, Seaford, and parts of Levittown. Levittown was the first suburb to be built after World War II, on land that was once potato fields. Most of the residents were Roman Catholic and of Irish or Italian descent. There were no black children among the 4,300 who attended school in the district at that time. Many students said the only knowledge they had of poverty and minorities was through books like the ones that were banned.

A *New York Times* reporter wrote that shopping malls were the only attractions in the area, which is a short ride from New York City. The lives of the people, the reporter noted, revolved around their homes and their schools.[13] This fact pleased many of the board members, who said the children needed to be protected from the harsh reality of the world.

Board member Martin, a father in his mid-30s and a New York City police officer at the time, said he was trying to protect children from the foul language on the streets. "When I was growing up, if you used language like that, you'd get your head cracked at home,"[14] he said.

Despite the protests, many people apparently agreed with the school board. In May 1976, the voters of the Island Trees school district reelected board members Richard Melchers and Louis Nessim.

A year later, when Martin ran for re-election, he continued to defend the board's action. He told a reporter that the school board was steering students "back to the basics" of reading, arithmetic, and discipline. Voters returned him to the board as well.

In response to the criticism, the board appointed a book review committee consisting of four Island Trees parents and four staff members to review the books.

The four parents were Donald Ferris, a former member of the board of education; Thomas Lane, a 1972 graduate of Island Trees High School; George O'Donnell, a letter carrier for the U.S. Post Office; and Carol Sachs, president of the Island Trees Parent-Teacher Association Council.

The teachers were Robert Amato, the high-school social studies teacher; Irving Carroll, the high-school principal; Charles Lipp, who taught high-school English; and Richard Segerdahl, another school principal.

The committee members read all the books but one, *A Reader for Writers*, because they were not able to find any copies of it. They met several times in June and July to discuss the books and to vote on their suitability.

At the end of July the committee recommended that five books, *Laughing*

Boy, *Black Boy*, *Go Ask Alice*, *The Fixer*, and *Best Short Stories by Negro Writers*, be kept in the school libraries. The committee said two books, *The Naked Ape* and *Down These Mean Streets*, should be removed. Committee members could not agree on the books *Soul on Ice* and *A Hero Ain't Nothing but a Sandwich*. They recommended parental approval be required to read *Slaughterhouse Five*, and they took no position on *A Reader for Writers*.

The board ignored the committee's recommendations and on July 28, 1976, voted to return *Laughing Boy* to the library and to require parental permission to read *Black Boy*. Board members voted to ban the remaining nine books from use in the schools. The board refused to say why they ignored the committee's recommendation, saying only that the books were "educationally unsound."

"It is not only our right but our duty to make the decision, and we would do it again in the face of abuse heaped upon us by the media," Ahrens said at the time.[15]

When the school year began again in the fall of 1976, the books were not on the shelves. The controversy continued.

On October 21, a group of residents formed the Right to Read Association of Island Trees and held their first meeting at the Island Trees Public Library. The meeting focused on the book-banning issue and included a speaker on censorship.

Meanwhile, the board also came under repeated criticism from the Island Trees High School student newspaper, the *Bulldog*. The newspaper's December 1976 edition contained several articles, editorials, and a cartoon on the issue. The newspaper's editorial writer called the ban "entirely improper." The writer also wrote that the ban reflected the board's belief that it was not accountable to anyone else.[16]

Another writer, Russell Rieger, said students of Island Trees High School

Students, community members, representatives of the NYCLU, and authors of the banned books meet at a gathering organized by Edna Yarris and other Island Trees residents opposed to book banning. Front, from left: student Glenn Yarris, Jeanne Lawlor, and author Piri Thomas. Back, from left: author Kurt Vonnegut, student Paul Sochinski, NYCLU lawyer Barbara Bernstein, and Justine Schacter, president of the Public Library Board.

were mature enough to choose their own books. Rieger called the ban an "infringement on our rights."[17]

By this time, parents who opposed the ban had contacted the New York Civil Liberties Union, an organization that helps people who believe their constitutional rights have been violated.

Barbara Bernstein, executive director of the Nassau County Chapter of the NYCLU, helped the parents organize their opposition to the ban. NYCLU officials explained how the parents could take the school board to court to force it to replace the books. Because the school board refused to end the ban, this appeared to be the next step.

CHAPTER THREE

Book **B**anners in **A**ction

*Boards of education . . . have, of course,
important, delicate, and highly discre-
tionary functions, but none that they
may not perform within the limits of the
Bill of Rights.*[1]

— Justice William Brennan
in *Board of Education v. Pico*

Schools are often the targets of book censors. In the past
two decades more and more parents have tried to restrict what their children
are reading in school.

Organizations from outside a school district often become involved in book
censorship cases. The cases often involve emotional pleas from the parents,
students, teachers, and school officials who are involved. Sometimes, violence
can erupt.

Kanawha County, West Virginia, is in the southwestern part of the state.
It is mostly rural, although it includes the state's capital city, Charleston. The
people who live in the county have a strong belief in God and in fundamentalist
religion.[2]

**A woman protesting textbooks in Kanawha County, West Virginia, sits on the curb
with her sign during a protest in 1974.**

In the spring of 1974 the county school board approved a list of 325 textbooks that would be used in the district's schools the next year. Alice Moore, the wife of a local minister and a member of the board, was not happy with the books. She said the books contained material that was disrespectful of authority and religion, destructive of social and cultural values, obscene, pornographic, unpatriotic, and violated individual and family rights.[3]

That summer county residents who agreed with Moore protested the books. Some said they contradicted the literal interpretation of the Bible; others said the books were "dirty." Some said that books by black authors would stir up trouble between blacks and whites in the county. One person objected to the story "Jack and the Beanstalk" because it implied that it was all right for poor people to rob and kill rich people.[4] Many of the county's ministers became involved in the matter, with 27 calling the books immoral. Ten of the ministers, however, supported use of the books.

That fall the situation grew more tense. Some parents kept their children out of school. Coal miners went on strike to protest the books. School buses were shot at, and a firebomb was thrown at an elementary school. Someone shot out the windows of the board of education building with a shotgun. The police arrested three members of the board and the superintendent, charging them with contributing to the delinquency of minors because they had approved the books. Things got so tense the superintendent closed the county's schools briefly to let people cool down.[5]

Alice Moore invited Mel and Norma Gabler to come to the county to speak. The Gablers, who are from Longview, Texas, run a textbook review company. They read schoolbooks to see if they contain material that is offensive to them or that challenges what they consider to be traditional American values. Like Moore, they did not like the books approved by the school board.

In an effort to end the matter, the school board approved new guidelines

Norma Gabler speaks before the Texas Board of Education. Gabler and her husband, Mel, help parents and groups seeking to ban books in schools.

for school book selection. The guidelines said books read in the schools should stress the importance of home and family and should encourage loyalty to the United States. The board also approved a book review committee of three parents and one teacher. The committee's job was to read and approve all suggestions for schoolbooks before they could be used in the schools.

Those steps were criticized by the National Education Association. The NEA, which represents teachers, said the guidelines would limit the exposure of students to different cultural and religious values.

By the time spring 1975 came, people had become tired of the controversy and lost interest in the issue. They were ready to end the fight. The charges against the school board members and the superintendent were quietly dropped. All the textbooks were accepted by the board. The battle was over.

To the Courts

Censorship cases are not always as dramatic or violent. Often the two sides take their dispute to the nation's courts for solutions. Judges have ruled differently in different cases. Some judges have said that school boards have the authority to make decisions about the books students can read in school. This could include removing books from libraries. Others have said that authority is limited and that school boards must have good educational reasons for removing books, that they cannot remove them just because they dislike the books or the ideas they present.

Many judges on both sides have said that the courts should not interfere with the decisions of local school boards unless questions about constitutional rights are at stake.

Those who argue against book banners say that censorship violates their First Amendment rights. The First Amendment is part of the United States Constitution in the section known as the Bill of Rights. It and nine other amendments were proposed and sent to the states for ratification by the first session of the First Congress. They were ratified on December 15, 1791.

The First Amendment guarantees the right to freedom of speech and religion, the right to assemble peaceably, and the right to petition the government for redress of grievances. It has been interpreted to mean that the government may not prevent people from practicing the religion of their choice or from reading, writing, and speaking what they choose. There are some limits. Supreme Court Justice Oliver Wendell Holmes wrote in 1919 that the government could prevent the use of words that would "bring about the substantive evils that Congress has a right to prevent."

As an example he wrote:

"The most stringent protection of free speech would not protect a man falsely shouting fire in a crowded theater and causing a panic."[6]

When a court makes a decision about book-banning cases, or any other case, that decision becomes a precedent that will help decide future cases. Judges who must decide a case look at the decisions made by past judges and courts in similar cases. Those decisions help guide the judge as he or she weighs the facts of a case. The judges who heard the *Pico* case relied on precedents in several cases.

"Pall of Orthodoxy"

One of the earliest school censorship cases surrounded not a book but a theory. In 1925 high-school biology teacher John T. Scopes was charged with violating an antievolution law in Tennessee. That law prohibited the teaching of Charles Darwin's theory of evolution. Darwin believed that humans evolved from lower life forms and apelike ancestors millions of years ago. Some people believed that theory contradicted the belief that God created the world and human life.

The case went to trial, and Scopes was convicted and fined. Although the fine was later reduced, the Tennessee law remained in effect until 1967.[7]

In 1968 a similar case was heard, but this time with a different result. An Arkansas high-school biology teacher named Susan Epperson objected to a state law. The law said if she used a textbook that included Darwin's theory of evolution, she could be fired. She filed a lawsuit against the state. The case, *Epperson v. Arkansas*, went to the Supreme Court, which ruled in 1968 that the law was unconstitutional because it violated the First and Fourteenth amendments. The Fourteenth Amendment requires that states respect the rights guaranteed in the Constitution.

The court's majority opinion noted that the First Amendment prevents school officials from "casting a pall of orthodoxy" over the classroom. This meant that school officials could not require teachers to teach one "official" version of a subject and ignore all others.[8]

The court ruling was also significant because for the first time it stated the court's reluctance to interfere in local matters. The Supreme Court justices said that the courts should not enter local school disputes unless the actions involve violation of constitutional rights.[9]

Constitutional Rights

In a 1943 case, *West Virginia State Board of Education et al. v. Barnette et al.*, the Court ruled that laws governing schools cannot violate students' constitutional rights. Walter Barnette was a parent and a Jehovah's Witness, a religious group that believes the law of God is higher than human laws. People who believe in this religion are not allowed to worship "graven images"—an idol carved in wood or stone.

Barnette's and other Jehovah's Witnesses' children had been expelled from school because they refused to salute the American flag and say the Pledge of Allegiance. They said this violated their religious beliefs. A state law required schoolchildren to say the pledge and salute the flag every day. Those who did not were called "insubordinate" and were expelled from school. If they were expelled, their parents could be charged by police and fined or sent to jail.

Barnette and other Jehovah's Witnesses sued the state board of education in federal district court. There the judge ruled that their children did not have to salute the flag or say the Pledge of Allegiance. The state board of education appealed the case to the Supreme Court. On June 14, 1943, the Court upheld the district court judge's ruling, relying on the free speech clause of the First Amendment. In its majority opinion the court wrote:

> No official, high or petty, can prescribe what shall
> be orthodox in politics, nationalism, religion, or
> other matters of opinion, or force citizens to
> confess by word or act their faith therein.[10]

This meant school officials could not force Jehovah's Witness children, or any children, to say the Pledge of Allegiance. This case was cited by the Court in its opinion on the *Pico* case.

Students' Rights

Another case, in 1969, reaffirmed that students have rights. Although it did not deal with book censorship, the case is often cited in book-banning cases.

During the 1967 holiday season several students in the Des Moines Independent Community School District wore black armbands to school to protest United States involvement in the Vietnam War. The students were ordered by the school principal to remove the armbands or face suspension. Most of the students followed the principal's order. But students John Tinker,

15, his sister, Mary Beth, 13, and Christopher Edkhardt, 16, ignored the warning and came to school wearing armbands. They were suspended and later sued the school district. The case was called *Tinker v. Des Moines.*

The district court and court of appeals ruled in favor of the school district. When the students appealed to the Supreme Court in 1969, they won. The majority opinion of the Court stated that students and teachers do not "shed their constitutional right to freedom of speech or expression at the schoolhouse gate." The Court went on to state that because there was no evidence of a serious discipline problem, the students had a right to wear the armbands.

School Board Authority

In March 1971, the Community School Board 25 in Queens, New York, voted to remove Piri Thomas's *Down These Mean Streets* from the high-school and junior high-school libraries. Residents of the school district said they were offended by Thomas's use of four-letter words and his detailed descriptions of sexual experiences, crime, and violence.

Several teachers, students, parents, a principal, and a librarian formed a group to oppose the removal. They called themselves the Presidents Council. They sued the school board, saying the removal of the book violated the First, Fourth, Fifth, and Fourteenth amendments. The case was called *Presidents Council v. District 25 Community School Board.*

The Fourth Amendment guards against the unreasonable seizing of a person's property, in this case, the book. The Fifth Amendment prevents the taking of property without due process. This means that before a governmental body can take property, it must hold a hearing of some sort.

The lower court upheld the school board's decision, saying that no constitutional rights had been violated. The Presidents Council appealed the decision, and in 1972 the U.S. Court of Appeals, Second Circuit, also upheld the school board's decision. Judge William Mulligan of that court agreed that no constitutional issues were involved. He also said the courts should not interfere in decisions of local school boards.

The Presidents Council group again appealed the decision, this time to the Supreme Court. But in November 1972 the Court refused to hear the case. It was a victory for the authority of the school board.

Students' Right to Know

In 1972 the school board of Strongsville, Ohio, refused to allow English teachers to use the books *Catch 22* by Joseph Heller and *God Bless You, Mr. Rosewater* and *Cat's Cradle* by Kurt Vonnegut in their classes. The board said the books were adult-oriented and unsuitable for use in a high-school classroom. Board members also approved two resolutions ordering the books removed from the school libraries.

Five families, including that of student Susan Lee Minarcini, sued the school board. The case became known as *Minarcini v. Strongsville City School District*. The district court judge ruled that the board had followed the proper procedure for making the selections and said that no constitutional rights had been violated because the books could be found outside the classroom.

The families appealed the decision. Appellate Judge George C. Edwards, Jr., said that although the school board might have the authority to approve or purchase textbooks, it could not remove books already purchased. On August 30, 1976, he voided the board's resolutions and ordered the books returned to the library shelves.

In his decision he wrote:

> A library is a storehouse of knowledge. When
> created for a public school, it is an important

privilege created by the state for the benefit of
students in the schools. That privilege is not
subject to being withdrawn by succeeding school
boards whose members might desire to winnow
the library for books the contents of which occa-
sioned their displeasure or disapproval.[11]

The school board appealed the decision, but the Supreme Court refused
to hear the case. This case is considered by some to be a victory for a student's
right to know.[12]

Refining the Precedents

A case in Chelsea, Massachusetts, in the mid-1970s helped to clarify
precedents set in two earlier cases and to strengthen the right of students to read
freely. In March 1976, at the same time the *Pico* case was unfolding, a member
of the Chelsea School Board objected to a book called *Male and Female under
18* that was in the school library. The board member, Andrew P. Quigley, said
a poem in the book called "The City to a Young Girl" contained sexual slang and
was improper for students to read. Quigley called an emergency meeting of the
school board and ordered School Superintendent Vincent McGee to remove the
book. Six weeks later the board voted to ban the book.

In reaction to this, several students and their parents, the school librarian,
and an English teacher formed the Right to Read Defense Committee of Chelsea
and sued the school board. The case was argued in district court in the spring
of 1978 before Judge Joseph L. Tauro. The Right to Read Committee said the
banning violated their First Amendment rights. The school committee disagreed, saying it had unlimited authority to remove books they did not like.
They cited the *Presidents Council* precedent to support their claim.[13]

In July 1978 Judge Tauro ruled in favor of the Right to Read Committee. He said that although school boards have authority to select books, their power to remove them is limited by the First Amendment. He said the *Presidents Council* case allowed school boards to remove books only if they were considered obsolete, irrelevant, or improperly selected in the first place. That was not the case here, Tauro said.

Judge Tauro also discussed the *Minarcini* precedent and how it applied to this case. He said the ruling in the *Minarcini* case prevented school boards from tampering with the contents of the school library based on their own social or political tastes. In his decision he wrote:

> The most effective antidote to the poison of mind-less orthodoxy is ready access to a broad sweep of ideas and philosophies. There is no danger in such exposure. The danger is in mind control.[14]

A Book Burning

A 1979 case reaffirmed the power of school boards to control what students read. The story began in July 1977 when the school board of Warsaw, Indiana, ordered the textbook *Values Clarification* banned from the school. The board objected to part of the book that posed questions about divorce, drugs, and premarital sex.

That fall the principal of the Warsaw high school ordered an English teacher not to use several books in her Women in Literature course, *Growing Up Female in America* and *The Stepford Wives*. The principal said he was concerned someone in the community might be offended by the books. The principal also told the teacher not to use *Go Ask Alice* and *The Bell Jar* by Sylvia Plath.

That December the Warsaw Senior Citizens Club burned copies of the *Values Clarification* textbook in an effort to show their support for the school board. In the spring the teacher's contract was not renewed. The board also fired another teacher who had criticized the board.

A year later a high-school student, Brooke Zykan, her brother, Blair, and their parents sued the school board. They said the board had violated their First and Fourteenth amendment rights by removing the books and firing the teachers. On December 3, 1979, the U.S. district court refused to rule on the case. The judge, Allen Sharp, said the board had not violated the student's constitutional rights.

The students appealed Sharp's decision to the U.S. Seventh Circuit Court of Appeals. On August 22, 1980, Judge Walter J. Cummings upheld Sharp's decision. Cummings based his decision on the *Presidents Council* precedent. He said that school boards may make decisions based on their own personal, social, political, and moral views.

A Similar Case

In the early 1980s, a case similar to the *Pico* situation occurred several hundred miles north of Long Island in Baileyville, Maine. There, Betsy Davenport, a 15-year-old student at Woodland High School, had checked out *365 Days* from the school library. The book, written by Ronald Glasser, is a collection of stories about soldiers wounded in the Vietnam War. When Davenport's mother, Carol, saw what her daughter was reading, she protested to the school board and asked the board to remove the book from the school.

On April 28, 1981, the board banned the book. Davenport and board members said they objected to the author's use of foul language spoken by the soldiers in the book.

Michael Sheck, an 18-year-old senior at the high school, sued the school board and Superintendent Raymond Freve, accusing them of violating the First and Fourteenth amendments.

The case was tried in U.S. district court in Bangor that December before Judge Conrad Cyr. Sheck and his lawyer, Roland Cole, argued that the language used by the author was important in relating the horrors of the Vietnam War. Sheck testified that students in the school frequently used the same words.

The lawyer for the school board said the banning was not meant to limit free speech, noting that students could find the book elsewhere in the area. The lawyer said the ban did not violate anyone's constitutional rights. He noted other court cases in which judges had said courts should stay out of local issues unless constitutional issues were at stake.

A month later, on January 22, 1982, Cyr ruled on the side of Sheck, saying the board's action may have violated the student's First Amendment rights. Cyr cited the *Minarcini* and *Right to Read* precedents in his decision.

The five Island Trees students who filed a lawsuit against their school board pose in front of the district's high school in February 1977. From left are seniors Russell Rieger, Glenn Yarris, Steven Pico, and Jacqueline Gold. At right is Paul Sochinski, who at the time was still in junior high school.

CHAPTER FOUR

Students Go to Court

Banning books whose ideas or language may be offensive is as primitive as killing the messenger with the bad news.[1]

**— Barbara Bernstein and
Alan Levine, NYCLU**

On January 4, 1977, the parents of five students from the Island Trees senior and junior high schools filed a lawsuit on behalf of their children against the school board in New York State Supreme Court in Mineola, Long Island.

The students filing the suit in the Island Trees case were Steven A. Pico, the president of the senior class; Jacqueline Gold; Russell Rieger; and Glenn Yarris. From the junior high school was Paul Sochinski. They ranged in age from 13 to 17.

Pico, Rieger, and Gold all wrote for the Island Trees High School student newspaper, the *Bulldog*. The students were represented by the New York Civil Liberties Union.

To file a lawsuit, there must be a plaintiff. A plaintiff is a person or group of people who claim their rights have been violated. The NYCLU chose the five students to be the plaintiffs. Because Pico was the most involved in the case, he was listed first on the lawsuit. The case became known as the "Pico lawsuit."

In their lawsuit, the students said school board members removed the nine books because particular passages in the books "offended their social, political, and moral tastes."[2] They said this was not a lawful reason for banning the books.

The lawsuit claimed the board had violated the students' First Amendment rights. It asked the court to declare the book removal unconstitutional. It also asked the judge to order the board to return the books to the library.

Ira Glasser, the executive director of the New York Civil Liberties Union at that time, called the book ban "part of an epidemic of censorship in New York and 11 other states directed by self-appointed vigilantes who do not have the insight to understand their educational mission."[3]

The school board had a different view. In a newspaper editorial written by the board, its members said they had the power to remove the books. They charged that the American Civil Liberties Union (ACLU) was trying to take control of the school. "Almost always these court decisions have resulted in the loss, to some degree, of the control of the schools by the people who fund them," the board members wrote.[4]

Lawsuit Moved

The state court system usually hears disputes that involve state or local laws, although sometimes they handle federal constitutional cases. Federal courts hear disputes that involve federal laws. They also hear disputes that involve questions about constitutional rights.

The NYCLU lawyers filed the suit in a state court even though they claimed the students' constitutional rights were violated. They did this because they feared the federal district court would rule against them. The federal court that served the Long Island area was the same one that had ruled in favor of the school board in the *Presidents Council* case in 1971.

But the school board wanted the lawsuit in a federal court. Federal District Court Judge George C. Pratt agreed with the school board. He said that since the students claimed their federal constitutional rights were violated, the lawsuit belonged in a federal court.

For two years the case remained unresolved while Judge Pratt weighed the arguments of the school board and of the students and the NYCLU. On August 2, 1979, Pratt issued his ruling. He agreed with the school board and dismissed the students' case without holding a trial.

In his decision, Pratt cited the reason for supporting the school board:

> The board acted not on religious principles but on its conservative educational philosophy, and on its belief that the nine books removed from the school library and curriculum were irrelevant, vulgar, immoral, and in bad taste, making them educationally unsuitable for the district's junior and senior high school students.[5]

Although the judge agreed that the board had removed the books because of their contents and called the decision "misguided educational philosophy," Pratt said that no constitutional rights had been violated. He relied on precedents set in two previous cases, *Presidents Council* and *Epperson*, which gave school boards the power to make decisions about school curriculum and books. Pratt's ruling stated:

> Noting that statutes, history, and precedent had

Three of the students who sued the Island Trees School Board in the *Pico* book-banning case, from left: Glenn Yarris, Paul Sochinski, and Steven Pico

vested local school boards with a broad discretion to formulate educational policy, the court concluded that it should not intervene in "the daily operations of school systems" unless "basic constitutional values" were "sharply implicated."[6]

Students Appeal

The students and the NYCLU disagreed. Believing a trial should be held to determine who was right, they appealed Pratt's decision to the United States Court of Appeals for the Second Circuit. This is a federal court that hears appeals of federal cases from the states of Connecticut, New York, and Vermont. They asked the higher court to decide if Pratt had made the correct decision in their case.

On February 6, 1980, three judges of the appeals court, Charles P. Sifton, Jon O. Newman, and Walter R. Mansfield, heard arguments from the NYCLU attorneys representing the students and from George Lipp, Jr., representing the school board.

The appeals court ruled 2 to 1 on October 2, 1980, that Pratt had not made the correct decision and ordered that a trial be held.

Judge Sifton, who wrote the decision for the court, said the book removal was "an unusual and irregular intervention in the school libraries' operations by persons not routinely concerned with such matters."[7] Sifton said that the school board's arguments for removing the books were not complete enough to make a judgment without holding a trial. He said the court needed to find out whether the books were as bad as the school board said, or if the board members were just uncomfortable with ideas in the books.

Judge Newman agreed with Sifton. Neither Newman nor Sifton cited any book censorship case precedents because they had not been asked to rule on the actual banning. The students had asked them to rule only on whether Pratt was correct to deny them a trial.

Judge Mansfield disagreed with Sifton and Newman, saying the evidence in the case was enough to support the board's argument. He wrote:

> The undisputed evidence of the motivation for the
> Board's action was the perfectly permissible
> ground that the books were indecent, in bad taste,
> and unsuitable for educational purposes.[8]

Judge Mansfield also said the board had acted "carefully, conscientiously, and responsibly after according due process to all parties concerned" when it made the decision to remove the books.

To the Supreme Court

The decision of the appellate court had left many questions that the school board and its lawyer found disturbing. The board decided to appeal its case to the Supreme Court. It would ask the Supreme Court to overrule the appellate court and allow Judge Pratt's decision to stand.

This was a big decision. The Supreme Court is the highest court in the nation. It usually hears cases only after they have been argued in lower courts. The Constitution makes the Court the final decision maker in cases. It is the highest interpreter of United States law. The decisions made by its justices can affect every person in the country.

Over the years the Court has made many famous decisions that affect the way we live today. One decision, *Brown v. Board of Education*, ended the segregation of black and white children in public school. Another decision, *Roe v. Wade*, made abortion legal across the country.

Members of the 1982 Supreme Court pose for an official portrait. Seated from the left are Thurgood Marshall, William Brennan, Jr., Chief Justice Warren Burger, Byron White, and Harry Blackmun. Standing from the left are John Paul Stevens, Lewis Powell, William Rehnquist, and Sandra Day O'Connor.

In 1990, the Supreme Court justices received more than 6,000 requests to hear cases. They actually issued opinions on only 121 of those. This number has risen each year, making the court's workload very heavy.

In most cases where people appeal lower court rulings to the Supreme Court, they submit a petition or writ of certiorari. This is a statement, in writing, outlining the reasons the Supreme Court should review the case. If the Supreme Court grants the certiorari petition, it will then hear the case. Four justices must agree to hear the case for certiorari to be granted.

The Court receives thousands of requests for certiorari each year, but it chooses only unusual or important cases. These can be cases that involve:

- Constitutional questions;
- Conflicting rulings on the law by different courts;
- A decision by a state court on a point of federal law.

George Lipp, Jr., the attorney for the school board, filed a brief on June 1, 1981, seeking certiorari from the Court. Briefs are the legal arguments lawyers use to support their cases. In them the lawyers discuss the facts of the case. They also note laws that support their case. They use the briefs to answer charges made by lawyers for the other side. The judges use the arguments in the briefs to help decide the outcome of the case.

In his brief Lipp pointed out:

1. The appellate court decision raised questions about the authority of a school board to determine what its students read and study.
2. The appellate court decision conflicted with the decisions of other appellate courts on similar issues.
3. The appellate court decision was divided.
4. The appellate court decision was wrong.

Lipp also noted in his brief that the case raised four questions:

1. How much does the Constitution restrict the

authority of a school board to remove library or classroom books?

2. Does the First Amendment give high-school students the right to sue a school board to force it to keep books on the library shelves?

3. Does a school board have to prove its removal of a book from the school library was based on educational reasoning?

4. Can books be removed from the school library for political reasons?

After receiving the school board's brief, the clerk of the Supreme Court reviewed the document to make sure it was complete, then assigned it docket number 80-2043. The docket number is the number that identifies the case. The "80" indicates the Court term in which it was filed. The Supreme Court's term runs from October of one year to October of the next. Thus, even though the brief was filed in 1981, it was part of the court's 1980 term.

The second number, 2043 in this case, indicates this was the 2,043rd case docketed in the court in the 1980 term.

The school board's petition for certiorari was 20 pages long and, like most briefs, typed. But some briefs received by the Court have been handwritten on prison stationery and filled with spelling and grammatical errors.[9] The justices give these briefs the same consideration they give the more "correct" briefs as they decide which cases to review.

To decide which cases the Court will hear, the justices meet in a conference room after being summoned there by a buzzer. There they shake hands and begin their deliberations. This is a private meeting. There is no one else in the room but the justices.

The justices work from a list of cases that the chief justice believes are important. The chief justice gives a brief review of each case. Then each justice, beginning with the senior associate justice, discusses the case, including whether he or she believes it should be heard.

On October 13, 1981, the justices decided the *Pico* case should be heard by the Court. Because the board of education was the petitioner (the party asking that the case be reviewed), the case became known as *Board of Education v. Pico.*

In Supreme Court cases, the petitioner has 45 days to file its briefs. The other side, the respondents, have another 30 days to file their briefs.

After being notified that the Court would hear the case, Lipp prepared a brief with the school board's arguments. The brief was 44 pages long and was filed on December 2, 1981. In it Lipp made these arguments:

> 1. The school board had the authority to deter-
> mine what books were suitable to be read by its
> students. By doing this, the school board was
> legally passing on the community's values to the
> students.
> 2. The board's removal of the books did not
> infringe on the students' First Amendment rights
> because the books could be found elsewhere in the
> community. Because of this, the courts should not
> attempt to interfere with the board.
> 3. The board's actions were not done without a
> good reason, and the board was not trying to
> prevent the students from reading ideas.

After Lipp filed his arguments, the NYCLU lawyers filed their own brief on January 5, 1982, explaining their case. Their brief was 36 pages long.

In it, the NYCLU attorney, Alan Levine, made these points:

> 1. The school board had violated the First Amendment when it banned the books. The board banned the books because the members disapproved of the ideas and values in them. By banning the books, the school board was trying to enforce "orthodoxy" and allow the students to learn only the things the board wanted them to learn. In the 1967 case *Keyishian v. Board of Regents*, the court ruled that "the First Amendment . . . does not tolerate laws that cast a pall of orthodoxy over the classroom."
> 2. Even though the books contained vulgar words, it was still unconstitutional for the school board to remove them from the library.

By now, everything was filed with the Court. The clerk of the Supreme Court notified the lawyers that oral arguments were set for March 2, 1982.

CHAPTER FIVE

Before the Justices

*I therefore view today's decision with
genuine dismay.[1]*

— Justice Lewis F. Powell
in *Island Trees vs. Pico*

Finally March 2, 1982, arrived, the day for which both
sides had long waited. Steven Pico was now 22 years old. He had graduated from
Island Trees High School and gone on to Haverford College, in Haverford,
Pennsylvania. His involvement in the case had changed his life. He was now
working for the National Coalition Against Censorship, an organization based
in New York that helps people and groups fight censorship.

Only one of the five students in the case was still in high school, Paul
Sochinski, the youngest of the group. He was a senior and would graduate that
June.

Of the seven school board members involved, five remained on the
board—Martin, Hughes, Fasulo, Melchers, and Nessim.

The lawyers and their clients—the original seven school board members
and Pico—crossed the stone-paved yard and climbed the marble steps at One
First St., NE, Washington, D.C., the Supreme Court building.

**NYCLU attorneys Barbara Bernstein, left, and Alan Azzara, center, speak with Steven
Pico on the steps of the U.S. Supreme Court in 1982.**

On either side of them stood a sculpture by artist James Earle Fraser. On the left was a seated woman, representing the contemplation of justice. On the right was a man, representing the guardian, or authority of law. Overhead, as everyone walked between the massive Corinthian columns, was the motto: "Equal Justice Under Law."

Inside, the parties crossed a floor of Alabama marble and entered the courtroom through a massive door made of white oak. There they stood on the red carpet, looking at the 24 columns of Italian marble surrounding the room and at the ceiling, 44 feet above them. Then they took their seats.

Moments later the bailiff cried, "Oyez!" The lawyers and their clients stood as the justices of the U.S. Supreme Court entered, their black robes flowing, and sat in the black leather chairs behind the tall, three-sided, polished mahogany wood bench.

Sitting on the left was John Paul Stevens, who had been appointed by President Gerald Ford in 1975. Next to him was William H. Rehnquist, named to the bench by President Richard Nixon in 1972. Next was Thurgood Marshall, who was appointed by President Lyndon Johnson in 1967. Sitting next to Marshall was William J. Brennan, Jr., appointed by President Dwight Eisenhower in 1956.

In the center seat sat the Chief Justice, Warren Burger, appointed by President Nixon in 1969. To Burger's left was Byron White, appointed by President John Kennedy in 1962. Next to him sat Harry A. Blackmun, appointed to the bench by President Nixon in 1970. Then came Lewis F. Powell, Jr., who was appointed by President Nixon in 1972. At the end sat Sandra Day O'Connor, the most recently appointed member of the court, by President Ronald Reagan in 1981.

It was an imposing sight for the lawyers and their clients, who were respectfully quiet as they readied themselves for their turn before the bench.

Justice Sandra Day O'Connor stands with Chief Justice Warren Burger on the steps of the Supreme Court building a few days before O'Connor was sworn in as an associate justice of the high court in 1981.

U.S. Supreme Court cases are heard in this courtroom. The justices enter through the velvet curtains and sit in the chairs behind the wooden divider.

Questions and Answers

The rules of the Court allow each lawyer 30 minutes to discuss the case and answer questions from the justices. Although this is not the most important part of the Supreme Court process, it is perhaps the most intimidating. The lawyer stands at a lectern before a pair of microphones. He or she is supposed to outline the important facts of the case and tie them together in a convincing argument. The justices may interrupt at any time with questions. This can be unnerving for a lawyer who has spent hours preparing a statement.

On the lectern are two lights, one red, one white. The lights are to let the lawyer know when his or her time is nearing an end. The lawyers may use notes to help them, but they are not supposed to use a prepared statement. During the 1974 term, the justices interrupted a lawyer who was reading his argument from a statement and reminded him of the rule.[2]

Court experts over the years have disagreed on the importance of oral arguments. Some say they are very important and help to clarify the significant points of the case. Other Court watchers disagree and say the justices have already made up their minds before the arguments are given.[3]

No matter what the justices may believe, the lawyers who present their arguments treat the occasion seriously. The lawyers in this case, George W. Lipp, Jr., for the school board and Alan Levine for the students, were no exception. They were ready.

When the clock over the heads of the justices read 12:58 P.M., the arguments began. Lipp spoke first because his client, the school board, was appealing the decision of the second circuit. Standing between the two microphones, Lipp began by introducing the case. He noted that it "involves the alleged right of five public school students to receive the contents of nine books removed from the Island Trees Public School libraries."

Seconds after he started, he was interrupted with a question from Chief Justice Burger, who wanted to know if it mattered to the school board what was in the books. Lipp began to answer, but Burger cut him off with another question: What if the board had banned the New Testament and the Constitution of the United States?

For the rest of his half-hour, the justices peppered Lipp with questions about the case, mostly about the facts of the book ban. They wanted to know how board members were elected and how school officials chose library books.

Lipp at one point said it was important for the school board to have the authority to transmit local community values to the students. "[The] ability to tailor local programs to local needs is healthy, and if it involves favoring certain values over others, it should not require the intercession of the federal judiciary," Lipp said.

Justice O'Connor wanted to know if school board members thought there were any limits on what they could remove. Lipp replied that the board would not try to ban all the books on a certain subject or all the books that reflected a certain viewpoint. He also noted that the board had banned only nine books out of more than 7,000 in the school library.

Lipp acknowledged, however, that the school board did not use any identifiable standards when it voted to remove the books. This concerned Justice Marshall, who asked repeated questions about the standards the school board had followed when it banned the books. Lipp said that standards would be difficult to set because "you are dealing with such imponderables as morals, social values, ethics."

Lipp was solemn as he spoke to the justices and answered their questions. But he and others in the room had to laugh when one of the justices questioned why the school board members objected to the books. "It couldn't be just vulgarity, because I have a sneaking suspicion that once or twice during a year there is some vulgarity in the schoolyard there," Justice Marshall said.

Then the light on the lectern turned red and Lipp was done. NYCLU attorney Alan Levine stepped to the microphones.

"Mr. Chief Justice," Levine said as he began his argument. "Schools, of course, do transmit values. Local school boards may, of course, give particular regard for the values of the local community that they serve. What we say here is that they may not ignore their obligation to observe and respect a diversity of values."

Shortly after Levine began to describe his case, he, too, was interrupted by questions. The justices were concerned about whether a school board could remove books without violating the Constitution. They were also concerned by Levine's and the appellate court's assertion that the motivation of the board members was important. This, the justices said, could require the courts to become more involved in local school decisions.

Levine said that the courts must sometimes consider the reasons for banning a book. He said if the courts do not get involved, school boards would have too much power and could violate people's constitutional rights. "I don't think that a school board can cloak its political concerns in the mantle of educational suitability," he said.

By this Levine meant that the school board had banned the books because they disagreed with the message in the books, not because the books were unsuitable for students.

Levine's time ended with a question from one of the justices who asked: "Of course, you say all of these books should go back on the shelves."

"That's correct. Thank you, Your Honor," Levine replied.

Then Chief Justice Burger asked Lipp if he wanted to rebut. This meant he could answer or correct statements that Levine had made.

Lipp replied, "Yes, I do, very briefly, Mr. Chief Justice."

Lipp said he wanted to correct Levine's statement that the board had banned the books for political reasons. He said one book—*A Hero Ain't Nothing but a Sandwich*—was banned because it was in "bad taste."

Then the justices wanted to know if the board could remove every book that had the word "ain't" in it. This caused everyone to laugh. After a few more questions, the lectern light turned red and Lipp was done.

Chief Justice Burger said, "Thank you, gentlemen. The case is submitted." The large clock over the justices read 2:05 P.M. The lawyers were done. Now the case rested in the hands of the nine justices.

The U.S. Supreme Court building in Washington, D.C.

CHAPTER SIX

Victory!

In brief, we hold that local school boards may not remove books from school library shelves simply because they dislike the ideas contained in those books.[1]

— **Justice William Brennan**
in ***Board of Education v. Pico***

On June 25, 1982, a little more than three months after the case had been argued, the Supreme Court handed down its decision, voting 5 to 4 in favor of the students. The justices ordered the case to be returned to the district court for a trial. This affirmed the decision of the court of appeals and overturned the summary judgment issued by Judge Pratt in 1979.

Ira Glasser, executive director for the American Civil Liberties Union, called the decision a "major victory." He said it was important because school boards all over the country were being pressured by groups to ban certain books that groups like PONY-U (Parents of New York, United) opposed.

School board member Martin called the ruling a defeat for every parent and school board in the country. He said school boards in the future would be afraid to make decisions and that board members would fear being taken to court by people angry with their decisions. Martin said later he believed that most of the people in the Island Trees community supported the school board's action. Martin repeated his assertion that students could still find the books in local bookstores or public libraries.

But Edna Yarris, the mother of one of the students who sued the board, said some students do not have access to public libraries or the money to buy books. "I don't believe that words have ever hurt anyone anywhere," Yarris said.[2]

The decision also pleased district librarian Irene Turin. Turin, who was the librarian when the board banned the books, said, "I'm just feeling happy. I can't believe it. I've been singing 'God Bless America' all day long."

The Deliberations

After the justices had heard the arguments of the lawyers in March, they had to decide the case. To do this, they followed a time-honored process the court has used for many years.

First each justice, working alone, reviews the facts of the case and the case law that relates to the situation. Then the justices meet privately in a conference to discuss the case. The most junior justice, in this case, Sandra Day O'Connor, is assigned to get materials for the other justices and serve as a messenger.[3]

The justices meet in an oak paneled, book-filled chamber next to the chief justice's suite. They sit in chairs around a rectangular table. Each chair has a metal plate with the name of a justice on it. No one else is allowed in the room.

Like the conference where the justices decide which cases will be heard, this one begins with a shaking of hands. This tradition symbolizes harmony and was begun in the 1880s.[4] Then the chief justice calls the first case to be decided and begins the discussion.

After he is finished, the senior associate justice speaks, followed by the rest

Irene Turin, head of the library department for the school district, left, signs a poster as Alice Childress, author of *A Hero Ain't Nothing But a Sandwich*, waits her turn. Turin, librarian when the school board removed books from the Island Trees school libraries, was especially happy with the Supreme Court decision in the case.

of the justices, in order of their seniority. The justices may speak as long as they wish.

In the conference, the justices discuss the case and argue for what they believe is the right decision. Usually these conferences are calm, but in some cases the justices become excited as they argue their opinions. Because these meetings are secret, we do not know what takes place during the discussion of specific cases.

After the justices have discussed the case, they vote. It takes a majority of the justices—five if all nine are participating—to decide a case.

The Decision

Once the justices have voted on a case, a decision is written. A decision is a reasoned argument that explains the ruling of the Court and how the justices arrived at that ruling. The decision also explains the legal precedents involved in the case.

According to Supreme Court tradition, the job of writing the opinion is assigned by the chief justice to an associate justice if the chief justice agrees with the majority decision. If the chief justice disagrees with the majority, the most senior associate justice assigns the writing task. In the *Pico* case, Justice Brennan, the senior associate justice in the majority, was assigned to write the opinion of the Court's majority.

In deciding the case, Brennan wrote, the court had two questions it had to decide: Did the First Amendment impose limitations on the school board's authority to remove books from the library? And if it did, did the book ban exceed those limitations?

When he wrote the decision, Brennan said:

1. The First Amendment does limit the school

board's authority to remove books from the
school library.
2. Judge Pratt was incorrect in dismissing the case
without a trial because there were questions about
whether the school board's action had exceeded
its authority.

Brennan was joined by Justices Blackmun, White, Stevens, and Marshall.
Justices Burger, Powell, Rehnquist, and O'Connor disagreed and filed dissenting opinions.

Brennan's 11 Points

Brennan made 11 points in the opinion he wrote:

1. Courts in the past have left the control of
schools to state and local governments such as
school boards. That control means the school
board can set a curriculum that promotes good
citizenship and reflects community values.
Brennan also said school boards can promote
respect for authority and traditional social and
moral values. He cited both the *Epperson* and
Tinker precedents on this point.
2. Although school boards have control over
school curriculum and educational policy, that
control must not violate constitutional rights, in
this case, the First Amendment. He noted this
precedent was set in the *Barnette* case.

Supreme Court Justice William J. Brennan, Jr., wrote the majority opinion in the *Pico* decision.

3. Students are entitled to constitutional rights while in school. Here Brennan cited the *Tinker* precedent.

4. The courts should not interfere in the daily operation of schools, unless constitutional issues are at stake. Again he cited the *Epperson* decision.

5. The right to receive information and ideas is part of the First Amendment, even though it is not directly stated in the Bill of Rights. Here Brennan cited several noneducational cases in which the court held that "the Constitution protects the right to receive information and ideas."[5]

6. The school library is especially appropriate as a place where students' First Amendment rights are recognized.

7. The school library is outside the "compulsory classroom environment," and, because of that, is not under the school board's absolute authority.

8. The school board cannot exercise its authority in a "narrowly partisan or political manner."[6] As an example, Brennan said a school board made up of Democrats could not order the removal of all books written by Republicans.

9. The school board's motivation for removing the books from the library was important to determine whether the students' constitutional rights had been violated. If the board removed the books because they objected to the ideas in them and

wanted to deny students access to those ideas, that would violate the First Amendment. Removing books for vulgarity would present a different case.

10. The school board cannot remove books from the school library simply because they dislike the ideas in those books. A board cannot use its power to enforce orthodoxy, that is, force students to learn only one view of politics, nationalism, or religion.[7] In making this point, Brennan noted the precedent set by the *Barnette* decision.

11. The students' lawsuit raised questions about the school board's motivations behind the book removal. Brennan wrote that the removal procedure was "highly irregular," and "ad hoc." By this he meant that the board's procedure was adopted for the specific purpose of removing those particular books.

Justice Blackmun agreed with Brennan, saying a school board could not remove books from a school library for the purpose of restricting access to political ideas or social perspectives.[8]

Justice White agreed with Brennan's final point, saying a trial should be held on the students' lawsuit. But he would not discuss the other points in the case. He said the case dealt with a "largely uncharted field," and that those issues should be brought out in a trial.[9]

Chief Justice Burger wrote the opinion of the four justices who disagreed with the majority. His opinion, in which Justices Powell, Rehnquist, and O'Connor joined, said the decision went "beyond any prior holding under the

First Amendment." He said the decision created a new constitutional right giving students control over school policy decisions.

Burger went on to say, "I categorically reject this notion that the Constitution dictates that judges, rather than parents, teachers, and local school boards, must determine how the standards of morality and vulgarity are to be treated in the classroom."

Like Brennan, Burger reduced the issues of the case to two questions. But his questions were different from Brennan's:

> 1. Who will control schools — local school boards
> or federal judges and teenage pupils?
> 2. Are morality, good taste, and relevance to
> education valid reasons for making decisions
> about the contents of a school library?

In arguing his case, Burger made these points:

> 1. Because the books could be found outside the
> school library, the school board ban did not
> prevent the students from reading them. Burger
> also said that the school was not obligated to
> provide access to the books.
> 2. For the school to transmit community values to
> the students, the board had to make decisions
> based on the views of its members. Under this
> reasoning, Burger said it would be permissible for
> a board to remove books that used vulgar lan-
> guage if board members concluded the language

was inappropriate for students.

3. There was no difference between removing a book and refusing to acquire one.

Justice Powell, a former local school board member who had also served on the Virginia State Board of Education, said in a separate opinion that he viewed the decision "with dismay." He said that resolving educational policy conflicts in the courts would "corrode the school board's authority and effectiveness."[10]

In his dissenting opinion, Justice Rehnquist disagreed with Brennan's concern over the motives of the school board members. Rehnquist said board members did not try to suppress ideas but made a decision based on their belief the books were educationally unsuitable.[11] To support his argument, Rehnquist quoted from the *Zykan* decision, the Warsaw, Indiana, case in which the local school board removed several books from the schools and fired two teachers. In that case, the appellate court ruled that it was "permissible and appropriate for local boards to make educational decisions based upon their personal, social, political, and moral views."

Rehnquist also questioned Brennan's assertion that students have a right to receive ideas, arguing that such a right was "wholly unsupported by our past decisions and inconsistent with the necessary selective process of elementary and secondary education."[12]

Rehnquist disagreed with Brennan's interpretation of the *Tinker* decision. While he agreed that the decision protected the constitutional right of students to express their opinions, he said it did not protect their access to ideas.

Rehnquist also argued that school libraries are not a separate entity from the classroom, as Brennan had stated. Because of this, the school board could retain control over books in the library, as it would over books in the classroom.

Justice William H. Rehnquist, one of the dissenters in the *Pico* case

And like Burger, Rehnquist said he saw no difference between removing a book and refusing to acquire one.

In the end, Rehnquist said the actions of the Island Trees School Board were "hard to distinguish from the myriad choices made by school boards in the routine supervision of elementary and secondary schools."[13]

While Justice O'Connor said she did not personally agree with the board's action, she said it was within their authority to remove the books. "If the school board can set the curriculum, select teachers and determine initially what books to purchase for the school library, it surely can decide which books to discontinue or remove from the school library so long as it does not also interfere with the right of students to read the material and to discuss it," she wrote.[14]

CHAPTER SEVEN

Freedom to **R**ead

*If you're spending the taxpayer's
money, you have to put up with
citizens, parents, and taxpayers
looking over your shoulder and
second-guessing your judgment.*[1]

— **Phyllis Schlafly**

After the Supreme Court ruling, 1,200 Island Trees parents asked the school board to end the fighting and return the books to the school library shelves. The board agreed to put the books back until it made a decision about whether it would take the case to trial.

In August 1982, the board voted not to go to trial. One board member said that a trial could have the effect of giving control of the school libraries to the courts. But the board did not give up entirely. Board members voted that school librarians should tell parents if their children checked out any of the nine books from the library.

The NYCLU challenged the policy. It argued that the policy violated the rights of all students in the school. In December 1982, the New York State attorney general ruled that the policy violated the state's law that guarantees the privacy of library records.

Finally, on January 26, 1983, the school board of the Island Trees Free Union School District No. 26 voted 4 to 3 to leave the books on the shelves. The three school board members who voted against the motion were Richard Melchers, Frank Martin, and Christina Fasulo, who almost seven years earlier had voted to remove the books in the first place.

Fasulo said her mind had not been changed by the events of the previous years. "Until the day I die, I refuse to budge on my position," she said. "Since when is it demeaning to take filth off library shelves?"

Board member Patrick Hughes, one of the original board members, voted in favor of leaving the books on the shelves. He said the issue was taking time away from other things the board needed to handle.

The case was over.

The *Pico* Precedent

Since it was decided in 1982, the *Pico* case has been cited by judges in more than three dozen lawsuits. Even though *Pico* was a book-banning case, it has been cited in many different kinds of cases.

Several judges have quoted Justice Brennan's argument that the First Amendment provides for the right to receive information. In the 1991 case *Student Press Law Center v. The Hon. Lamar Alexander, Secretary, Department of Education and U.S. Department of Education*, a group sued the U.S. Department of Education, claiming that a 1974 government act that prevented colleges and universities from making certain student information public was unconstitutional.

That year the Department of Education had threatened to withdraw federal funds from several universities that allowed the names of students in their campus police crime reports to be published in newspapers. The Student Press Law Center in Washington, D.C., claimed the act violated the First Amendment right to freedom of speech. Among the arguments they cited was Justice Brennan's claim that the First Amendment protects the right of people to receive information and ideas.

In the *Pico* decision, Brennan had written:

> The right to receive information and ideas is an inherent corollary of the rights of free speech and press that are explicitly guaranteed by the Constitution.[2]

Other judges have used the *Pico* decision differently. In 1992, a U.S. district court judge in New York cited *Pico* when she dismissed a case by students who claimed their school had violated their rights. The case was *Sanford Grimes and Janelle Grimes v. Lauro Cavazos, Secretary of Education, U.S. Department of Education.*

Sanford and Janelle Grimes had claimed the school system was culturally biased against African-American students. Judge Kimba Wood ruled against the students. In her decision, Judge Wood noted that Justice Brennan had written in *Pico* that the federal courts should not interfere in local school decisions unless constitutional issues are at stake. Wood said the students' rights had not been violated.[3]

Two Supreme Court justices cited *Pico* when they voted in the 1987 case *Edwards v. Aguillard* that involved the teaching of evolution in Louisiana schools. In 1981 Louisiana passed a law that required the teaching of the biblical story of creation along with the Darwinian theory of evolution. When the case came before the Court, the justices ruled 7 to 2 that the law was unconstitutional because it violated the part of the First Amendment that prevents the government from establishing an official religion.

Justice Brennan, who wrote the decision, repeated one of the points he made in the *Pico* decision. He wrote that states should have the power to control schools, but that control must still respect the rights protected by the Constitution.

Justice Powell agreed with the decision, but also repeated the same statement he made in the *Pico* case:

> I adhere to the view that the states and locally
> elected school boards should have the responsibil-
> ity for determining the educational policy of the
> public schools.[4]

A Setback

When the Supreme Court ruled on the *Pico* case in 1982, one author called it "one of the most significant First Amendment decisions to be rendered by the Supreme Court in the past two decades."[5] Many believed it offered students a greater right to read what they wished.

But a Supreme Court ruling in 1988 cast doubt on that right. The case involved the Hazelwood East High School in St. Louis. In May 1983 the school's principal, Robert Reynolds, ordered two articles removed from the student newspaper, the *Spectrum*. One article was about pregnant teenagers. The other was about how divorce affected children. The principal said the articles were not appropriate reading for students.

Three students who worked on the newspaper sued the school. They said the principal's action had violated their First Amendment rights.

In 1988 the case made its way to the Supreme Court. In a 5 to 3 decision,

Supreme Court Justice Lewis F. Powell

the Court sided with the school. Only eight justices voted because a vacancy was created when Justice Lewis F. Powell resigned from the Court earlier that year. The spot had not been filled when the Court heard the case in October 1987.

In its decision the Court wrote that school officials may censor reading material for students if they believe the material is too advanced for the students.[6]

In the majority opinion, Justice Byron White wrote:

> We hold that educators do not offend the First
> Amendment by exercising editorial control over
> the style and content of student speech in school-
> sponsored expressive activities so long as their
> actions are reasonably related to legitimate peda-
> gogical concerns.[7]

Since then, many school officials have cited the *Hazelwood* decision when they prevent students from reading certain material, according to Leanne Katz, executive director of the National Coalition Against Censorship. "The federal courts are not the place to turn in order to ensure that there are broad educational freedoms in the schools," Katz said.

Some disagree and say the *Pico* decision still provides a guideline for school officials who are considering censoring certain reading materials. Among them is NYCLU attorney Arthur Eisenberg, who took part in the *Pico* case. He said the *Hazelwood* case involved issues about students' rights to free speech in school. Those issues are different from book-banning issues.[8]

Religion in the Schools

In addition to protecting the right of speech, the First Amendment protects the right of people to practice the religion of their choice. The amendment prevents the government from establishing an official religion. The courts have interpreted this to mean that public schools cannot teach religion.

Since the *Pico* case, some book-banning cases have involved religious issues. Often these cases are started by parents with strong religious beliefs who want schools to include religion in classroom lessons. One case began in 1983, when seven Christian Fundamentalist families sued the Hawkins County, Tennessee, school system. The case was *Mozert v. Hawkins County School System*.

The parents in the case objected to a textbook series their children were required to read. They said the series, published by Holt, Reinhart & Winston, was anti-Christian and taught witchcraft and disobedience to parents.[9] They also argued that the course violated the law against teaching religion in school. The course, the parents said, taught "secular humanism," which they argued was a form of religion.

The lower court agreed with the parents and said the students did not have to take the course. The school system appealed the case. In 1987 the appellate court reversed the lower court's decision. In the decision, Chief Judge Pierce Lively ruled that the course did not require the students to change their religious beliefs and so did not violate their constitutional rights.[10]

In another case, *Smith v. Board of School Commissioners of Mobile County*, a group of Christian Fundamentalist parents asked that 44 textbooks be banned from the classrooms of Alabama. As in the Tennessee case, the parents said the books taught secular humanism. The parents defined secular humanism as a "human-centered philosophy that amounted to an anti-Christian religion."[11]

The district court judge, W. Brevard Hand, sided with the parents and ordered the books banned on March 4, 1987. The state board of education

A Mobile, Alabama, high-school student turns over a banned history book to two school book-room workers in March 1987 after the book was banned from Alabama public schools by order of U.S. District Court Judge W. B. Hand. He ruled that the book teaches godless "secular humanism."

appealed the decision, and five months later the Eleventh Circuit Court of Appeals reversed the district court judge's ruling.

The battle over what students read in school continues. If anything, censorship attempts have increased since *Pico* was decided.

In 1991, a survey done by People for the American Way reported 348 cases where parents or groups of people had attempted to have books banned from schools. This number was the highest in the ten years the group had been surveying schools.[12] People for the American Way is a group that fights for the protection of First Amendment rights.

The same survey also found that many of the people who tried to have books removed from schools were successful. According to the survey, in 41 percent of the challenges, the books were either removed or student access to them was restricted.[13]

People who try to ban books have many reasons. Some, like the parents in Tennessee and Alabama, say certain books offend their religion. Others object to books that contain profanity or have sexually suggestive titles. In one case a school board voted to ban the book *Making It with Mademoiselle*, because of its title. The board quickly ended the ban when they learned the book was about sewing projects.

Parents often object to adolescent novels that deal with sex. Many have objected to books by author Judy Blume, who writes about young people, because the characters in Blume's books often deal with questions about sex. A 1993 case involved the Judy Blume book *Forever*. The book was reviewed by a committee at the Rib Lake (Wisconsin) High School at the request of the school's principal.

The book, which was in the high-school library, tells about a high-school senior's decision to have sexual intercourse with her boyfriend. It was removed by the school's principal, Paul Peterson, who saw a student reading it in the high-school cafeteria. After glancing at the book, the principal ordered the student to bring the book to his office. There he took the book from the student and ordered it reviewed.

The school board voted in the summer of 1993 to put the book on a restricted shelf in the library. In order for students to read it, their parents have to call the librarian and give their permission.

Ruth Dishnow, the school librarian who led the fight against the book's removal, was named civil libertarian of the year in 1994 by the American Civil Liberties Union of Wisconsin Foundation.

In the spring of 1994, a school board member in the New York City school system proposed to ban several books from libraries in the District 24 system. The board member, Frank Borzellieri, said the books prevented students from taking pride in being American.

The books included a biography of the slain civil rights leader Martin Luther King Jr. Other books on his list were *I Hate English*, a book about a Chinese girl's struggle to learn English, and *Jambo means Hello, the Swahili Alphabet*, a picture book with Swahili words. Borzellieri said students shouldn't have to learn about other cultures.

School officials supported the books, saying they were "educationally appropriate" and that they belonged in the school libraries.

Sometimes the objection goes beyond an individual book to include a whole school course. For instance, some parents have objected to drug and sex education courses. Others have objected to courses that study the values of society. Students taking these courses are sometimes required to study the values they live by and to question those values.

Other parents object to school courses about pagan cultures and different ethnic groups, and to books or courses that question the authority of parents.

Those who support censorship in the schools often argue that parents

School librarian Ruth Dishnow speaks at an ACLU banquet after being named civil libertarian of the year by the ACLU of Wisconsin Foundation. She was honored for her efforts to keep Judy Blume's book *Forever* on the library shelves.

have the right to control what public schools teach their children. Some parents with strong religious beliefs argue that books used by schools should teach children the values they consider important. Others object to the way certain books portray women or minorities. For example, some people have objected to the book *The Adventures of Huckleberry Finn* by Mark Twain. They say the book is racist because it refers to Jim, a black man, as a "nigger."

Those who oppose censorship say students need to see many different views of a subject, even if some of those views contradict what the students or their parents believe.

In its "Freedom to Read" statement, the American Library Association argues against censorship. A portion of the statement says:

> Parents and teachers have a responsibility to prepare the young to meet the diversity of experiences in life to which they will be exposed, as they have a responsibility to help them learn to think critically for themselves. These are affirmative responsibilities, not to be discharged simply by preventing them from reading works for which they are not yet prepared.[14]

Source Notes

Introduction

    1. Richard Hansen, *The First Freedom*, edited by Robert B. Downs (Chicago: American Library Association, 1960), p. 15.

    2. Donald J. Rogers, *Banned: Book Censorship in the Schools* (New York: Julian Messner, 1988), p. 3.

    3. William Noble, *Book-Banning in America* (Minneapolis: Paul S. Eriksson, 1990), p. 34.

    4. Donna A. Demac, *Liberty Denied: The Current Rise of Censorship in America* (New York: PEN American Center, 1988), p. 9.

Chapter One

    1. Newsletter of the Island Trees School Board (March 1976).

    2. Richard Morrow memo to school board (Feb. 27, 1976), *Pico* case file.

    3. Ruth Marcus, "Censorship in the Schools," *The National Law Journal* (May 25, 1981), p. A111 in the *Pico* case file.

    4. Ibid., p. A114 in the *Pico* case file.

Chapter Two

    1. *New York Times*, April 4, 1976, sec. 21, p. 4.

    2. *New York Times*, March 20, 1976, p. 31.

    3. Ibid.

    4. *New York Times*, March 27, 1976, p. 24.

    5. Ibid., March 28, 1976, sec. 21, p. 1.

    6. Affidavit of Richard Ahrens, *Pico* case file, appendix C.

    7. Newsletter of the Island Trees School Board (March 1976).

    8. *New York Times*, April 4, 1976, sec. 21, p. 4.

    9. Ibid.

    10. Ibid., March 28, 1976, sec. 21, p. 16.

11. Island Trees School Board press release, from *Pico* case file, appendix C.

12. Affidavit of Richard Ahrens, *Pico* case file, appendix C.

13. *New York Times*, May 22, 1977, p. 21.

14. *New York Times*, March 28, 1976, p. 21.

15. *New York Times*, July 29, 1976, p. 37.

16. *The Bulldog*, December 10, 1976, p. 2.

17. Ibid., p. 4.

Chapter Three

1. *Board of Education v. Pico*, 102 S. Ct., p. 2807.

2. Rogers, p. 17.

3. Ibid., p. 18.

4. Ibid., p. 20.

5. Ibid., p. 21.

6. *Encyclopaedia Britannica* (Chicago: Macropaedia, 1991), vol. 15, p. 625.

7. Ibid., p. 4.

8. Ibid., p. 7.

9. *Epperson v. Arkansas*, supra 393 US, p. 104.

10. *West Virginia State Board of Education et al. v. Barnette et al.*, 63 S. Ct., p. 319.

11. Henry Reichman, *Censorship and Selection: Issues and Answers for Schools* (New York: American Association of School Administrators and American Library Association, 1988), p. 120.

12. Rogers, p. 35.

13. Ibid., p. 42.

14. Ibid., p. 43.

Chapter Four

1. *Newsday*, Jan. 11, 1977, as found in *Pico* case file.

2. *Board of Education v. Pico*, 102 S. Ct., p. 2804.

3. *New York Times*, Jan. 5, 1977, sec. 2, p. 3.

4. *Newsday*, Jan. 11, 1977, as found in *Pico* case file.

5. *Pico v. Board of Education*, 474 F. Supp. 392.

6. Ibid., Supp. 395.

7. *Pico v. Board of Education*, 638 F.2d., p. 414.

8. Ibid., p. 419.

9. *The Supreme Court at Work* (Washington: Congressional Quarterly, 1988), p. 68.

Chapter Five

1. *Board of Education v. Pico*, 102 S. Ct., p. 2822.

2. *The Supreme Court at Work*, p. 69.

3. Ibid.

Chapter Six

1. *Board of Education v. Pico*, 102 S. Ct., p. 2810.

2. *New York Times*, June 27, 1982, sec. 4.

3. *The Supreme Court at Work*, p. 73.

4. Ibid.

5. *Board of Education v. Pico*, 102 S. Ct., p. 2808.

6. Ibid., p. 2800.

7. Ibid., p. 2814.

8. Ibid., p. 2816.

9. Ibid., p. 2822.

10. Ibid., p. 2829.

11. Ibid., p. 2830.

12. Ibid., p. 2835.

13. Ibid.

14. Ibid.

Chapter Seven

1. David L. Bender and Bruno Leone, *Censorship: Opposing Viewpoints* (New York: Greenhaven Press, 1988), p. 138.

2. *Student Press Law Center v. The Hon. Lamar Alexander, Secretary, Department of Education and U.S. Department of Education*, 715 F. Supp. 73.

3. *Sanford Grimes and Janelle Grimes v. Lauro Cavazos, Secretary of Education, U.S. Department of Education*, 786 F. Supp. 1184.

4. *Edwards v. Aguillard*, 482 US 605, p. 81.

5. Reichman, p. 74.

6. Demac, p. 21.

7. Ibid.

8. Interview with Arthur Eisenberg, NYCLU, by author (May 11, 1993).

9. "Books on Trial, Survey of Recent Cases," National Coalition Against Censorship 1991, p. 11.

10. Ibid.

11. Ibid., p. 6.

12. *Congressional Quarterly* (March 1993).

13. Ibid.

14. Bender and Leone, p. 142.

Further Reading

American Library Association Office for Intellectual Freedom. *Intellectual Freedom Manual*. Chicago: American Library Association, 1983.

Association for Library Service to Children. *Intellectual Freedom for Children*. New York: American Library Association, 1984.

Bender, David L. and Leone, Bruno. *Censorship: Opposing Viewpoints*. New York: Greenhaven Press, 1988.

Berger, Melvin. *Censorship*. New York: F. Watts, 1982.

Bosmajian, Haig A. *The Freedom to Read*. New York: Neal-Schuman Publishers, 1987.

David, Andrew. *Famous Supreme Court Cases*. Minneapolis: Lerner Publications Co., 1980.

Demac, Donna A. *Liberty Denied: The Current Rise of Censorship in America*. New York: PEN American Chapter, 1988.

Dority, Barbara. *School Censorship: An Emergency Response Manual*. Washington, D.C.: National Education Association, 1989.

Facklam, Margery. *The Trouble with Mothers*. New York: Clarion Books, 1989.

Hentoff, Nat. *The Day They Came to Arrest the Book*. New York: Delacorte Press, 1982.

Jenkinson, Edward B. *Censors in the Classroom: The Mind Benders*. New York: Avon Books, 1979.

Meltzer, Milton. *The Bill of Rights: How We Got It and What It Means*. New York: Thomas Y. Crowell, 1990.

Reichman, Henry. *Censorship and Selection: Issues and Answers for Schools*. New York: American Association of School Administrators and American Library Association, 1988.

Rogers, Donald J. *Banned: Book Censorship in the Schools*. New York: Julian Messner, 1988.

Taylor, C. L. *Censorship*. New York: F. Watts, 1986.

West, Mark I. *Trust Your Children: Voices Against Censorship in Children's Literature*. New York: Neal-Schuman Publishers, 1988.

Index